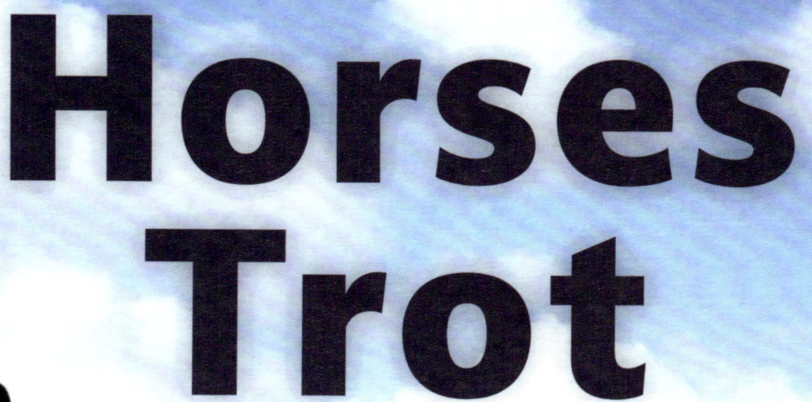

Horses Trot

Written by Michèle Dufresne

PIONEER VALLEY EDUCATIONAL PRESS, INC.

Look at the **horse**.
The horse has a lot
of spots!

This horse is an Appaloosa. These horses have been used in many movies.

A horse can trot, run, and **jump**.

Clip-clop, clip-clop! Look at the horse trot to the pond.

A trot is a bit faster than a walk but not as fast as a canter, which is a horse's run. A gallop is very, very fast.

The horse stomps his **hoof**. Plop! The horse's hoof went into the mud.

A horse's hooves are built to support the very heavy weight of the horse but are also light for running.

The horse comes
to a **fence**.
He stops.
Will he jump?

Horses can jump because of their powerful hindquarters. Some types of horses make great jumpers, whereas others are better at different skills, like pulling or endurance riding.

The girl taps the horse with a crop.

Up, up, up went the horse!

A riding crop is used to encourage horses to move. It should only be used with a very light touch.

glossary

horse

jump

hoof

fence